Letters 2 My Son

A Father's Journey of Self-Discovery and Healing

Sedrik Newbern

ONE11

One11 Publishing
872 S Milwaukee Ave, Suite 195
Libertyville, IL 60048

www.one11publishing.com

Publisher: Sedrik Newbern
Editor: Flora Brown
Cover Designer: Scott Ventura

Printed in the United States of America
First Edition: June 2017

Author's Note
This book is based on my life experiences for learning and teaching purposes only.

ISBN Paperback 978-0-9982892-2-9
ISBN Digital 978-0-9982892-3-6

One11 Publishing is an imprint of
Newbern Consulting Group, LLC.

Dedication

This book is dedicated to my amazing son. You have taught me so much about life and myself since I first held you in my arms. I am so thankful to God for giving me the gift of you my son.

I love you to infinity!

Contents

Acknowledgements

Matthew, I thank God every day for you. I thank Him for giving me the opportunity to be your dad. You inspire me to be great. You make me so proud. You challenge me in ways you may never understand. You give my life purpose and meaning.

To my wife, Denise, thank you! Your spirit, compassion, and love for others make me want to be a better man each and every day. Thank you for your continued prayer, patience, support, and willingness to unselfishly share me with others so that I can live out my passion and share the gifts God has given me. You are truly the wind beneath my wings.

Sam, thank you for always being there for me! We have been like brothers from the day we met over 30 years ago. As I look over my life, you have been by my side for many of the most memorable moments both good and bad. Your friendship and counsel is truly appreciated. As you know, this project has been on my heart for a couple of years. Thanks to you and your persistency, this book is now a reality.

I want to thank my family and friends for all of your support and encouragement.

To my wife, Denise Newbern; business manager, Samuel Watkins; consultant, DeShana Johnson; editor, Flora Brown; graphic designer, Scott Ventura; thank you all for the prayer, time, creativity, patience and support on this project.

Introduction

I have had the honor of being a dad to the most amazing son in the world. True, there are other dads and sons out there who feel they carry the same title. I'm not here to debate that issue. In fact, the reason I have written this book is to increase my competition for the title.

If you have read my other projects, you would know that my past did not set me up for a successful run at parenthood. My parents divorced when I was a year old, so statistically, I was destined to repeat the cycle of broken relationships.

However, I've been blessed with the gift of a son, Matthew. This young man has given me purpose and taught me so much about myself since the day he was born.

This book is a collection of special moments and insights I uncovered in my journey of self-discovery and healing as a new father. It is written as letters to my son describing the details of the moments as well as my thoughts and emotions.

It is my dream that more men see the title of dad as their greatest accomplishment. I want more men to discover that their true purpose is being a father and role model to their children and other young people who look to them as surrogate fathers. It is my hope that my experiences as a new dad and the meaning I found in those moments will inspire other men to look at their lives as meaningful to their children. I also hope that these moments inspire men who grew up without their fathers to face their fears and know that God has equipped them with the resources and support they need to be great parents and build a great foundation for their children.

As I continue to work through my fatherhood journey, I find great comfort and support in my faith and the community of men like myself trying to be great dads. I hope that this book brings more men together across the world to break the cycles of brokenness and show unconditional love to all children.

Son's Day

"Because of you son, every day is a Happy Father's Day."
~ Sedrik Newbern

Every year I celebrate Father's Day, I am convinced there should be a Son's Day too. You have made such an amazing impact on my life since the day I found out that mommy was pregnant!

On the day you were born, I was no longer the same. My sense of responsibility increased. My drive to be successful intensified. My passion to make a difference in the world flourished. My ability to love unconditionally took on a whole new dimension. All of this happened when I held you in my arms for the first time.

I want to share with you the moments that may seem insignificant to some but were, in fact, monumental for me.

I have enjoyed our journey together and all that you have taught me about myself. I can't wait to see where God takes us next!

Dad Means

"Becoming a dad means you have to be a role model for your son and be someone he can look up to." ~ Wayne Rooney

There's nothing I enjoy more than being a dad. Just to hear you call me dad (except when you're begging for another toy or video game) still makes me smile. The title of Dad means more to me than you know.

To begin to understand what this means, you have to know that my parents divorced before I was a year old. I grew up with my dad living over 2,000 miles away. I always wanted to have kids, but I had this fear that I would repeat the cycle. So as you can imagine, when the ultrasound tech said, "It's A Boy," I was filled with mixed emotions. These seven letters scared me and changed my life forever.

On one hand, I was excited beyond belief. After mom and I had decided to start a family, it took us over 9 months to actually get pregnant. This was very discouraging and frustrating for both of us. The doctors had warned us of a potential high-risk pregnancy or even infertility because of our age. When conception didn't happen right away, we began to think we would not be able to have children. Then it happened! We got the long awaited news that mom was pregnant.

When we found out that we were having a son, I was both happy and scared to death. Now I would have the opportunity to be the dad to you that I always wanted during my childhood. On the other hand, I questioned whether I knew how to be a father. Would I be there to watch you grow up? Could I be the example for you that every young man needs?

Once you were born, those fears soon became real. Sleepless nights worrying about providing for our family and giving you the foundation you would need to be successful consumed me. Then I realized that I had the best mentors and role models for fathers when I grew up. I began to reflect on how those men carried themselves and the impact they had on my life. I also had a great relationship with my dad and stepdad, so I talked with them to get advice and encouragement. Being a dad would not be as difficult as I thought.

Soon I realized, that I was more than just a dad to you son. When I began to coach your sports teams and volunteer at your school, I realized that I was a surrogate father for so many young people growing up without their dads. I was also breaking stereotypes of African American fathers for these children and their families. I had lost my old identity, and my name was no longer important. I was now known as Matthew's dad and I had gained an identity that gave my life meaning.

That's when it hit me! Being a Dad is a tremendous blessing. God chose me for this role because He knew that I had the experiences, passion, and potential that qualified me for the title and the responsibilities that came with it.

My son, you are by far the greatest accomplishment in my life. You inspire and challenge me each and every day. I know you think I am a superhero, but you are truly my superhero. You have saved me from my fear and helped me strive to be the best dad I can be, and dad to so many other kids. Thank you, son!

First Poop

"In many ways, changing your first poopy diaper was symbolic of wiping away the crap from my past." ~ Sedrik Newbern

After you were born, the nurses checked on us constantly. It was an additional comfort and needed support for me because we didn't have our family with us when you were first born. Mom and I were a long way from home, so we were on our own with you for the first couple of weeks. To have family around to help us would have been great, but I believe those weeks before the family arrived allowed us to bond as a family and enjoy you when you were first born.

I had no idea what a newborn needed or what we would encounter in those first few hours, days, and weeks. I would constantly ask the nurses questions to make sure we were doing this whole parenting thing right. Of course, the nurses would smile and patiently answer all my questions. They would always say, "Don't worry, you can't break him. Babies are very flexible and resilient."

The first day, they would come into the room and asked if you had a bowel movement yet. The first couple of times, I didn't think anything of it. However, the third time made me wonder if there was an issue or something significant related to the first poop. They explained among other things how the first bowel movement would indicate that his system was working properly and that it might take a while before it would happen.

Later that evening, it happened. Mom checked your diaper and discovered a little surprise was waiting for us. That's when I heard the magic words, "Do you want to change him?" But of course, I wanted to change the first diaper. I wanted to prove to mom that I was a soldier and not afraid to do the dirty work. I wanted to show that I was going to be involved in every aspect of raising you. I also didn't want mom to get out of bed after all she had been through. She had just delivered a baby, so changing a diaper was the least I could do to allow her to stay in bed and rest.

I took you from mommy's chest and laid you on the hospital bassinet the nurses used to bring you back and forth from our room to the nursery. You looked up at me as if you were thinking, *Dad what are you about to do to me?* I was so careful and gentle. I didn't want to hurt and contaminate your belly button. I also didn't want to break your leg or drop you. Yes, I was terrified!

As I removed the diaper to begin cleaning up the little surprise you gave us, I had an interesting experience. I started thinking about my life and what led up to that moment. How challenged my childhood was. How empty I felt as a kid without my dad. How scared I was when I found out we were having a baby and even more terrified knowing that my baby was a boy.

Now here I stood changing your diaper. The innocence in your face convicted me at that moment. I said to myself, "I have to be the best dad I can be for this little guy. I have to show him how to respect mom and all women. I have to show him by my example how to be a man, love others, and give unconditionally to those who are in need." As I felt the pressure of being a dad starting to overwhelm me, I heard mom say, "What does it look like?" I'll spare you the detail, but that was what I needed to bring me back to earth. I wiped your bottom, put the new diaper on and attempted to swaddle you with the blanket.

In many ways, changing your first poopy diaper was symbolic of wiping away the crap from my past. With a firm but gentle wipe, I cleaned your bottom. At the same time, I saw my future and the responsibility I would have as a father. I also saw this as a symbol of wiping away my past. I saw the opportunity to break the curse of divorce and broken families finally. I could be for you what I always wanted as a child. I could be the change I wanted to see not only for my son, but for so many other children.

That first year, I changed a bunch of diapers, but none quite as special as that first diaper.

Buckle Up

"I just want to protect you from everything that hurts you. I want you safe and happy." ~ Unknown

When the nurse said we could leave the hospital, I panicked. Would I remember all the stuff needed to take care of you? Did I know how to swaddle you in the blanket to keep you safe and comfortable? Was mom comfortable with feeding you enough to leave the support of the nurses? What if you stopped breathing, what would I do? Would I know what to do?

These were the thoughts I had in the elevator on my way to the car. It was a cold January morning in Northern VA with a few mounds of snow pushed into the corners of the hospital parking lot. As I sat in the car letting the engine run for a minute, I felt anxious. The fact that we were leaving the hospital meant that I no longer would have the help we had grown so comfortable with over the last few days in the hospital.

Then I looked in the rearview mirror and saw the car seat I had strapped in the backseat. Was it secure enough? Was it too big? You were so little that I didn't know if you would even fit in the carrier. Would you be warm and comfortable? Was there enough cushion in the carrier? Then I realized that I had left you and mom at the door waiting for me to bring the car around.

I snapped out of it and drove up to the door and rushed in with the carrier. Your mom was holding you snuggly in her arms, and you were sound asleep. Both of us struggled just to get you in the carrier and buckled in without waking you up... we didn't know at that time how sound you would sleep.

After a few minutes of stress, we got you buckled in the carrier which I then sat down on the base. Since I didn't hear a click, I removed the carrier and reattached it at least three times trying to make sure it was secure. I was so afraid that I would not attach the car seat properly and something would happen to you because of it.

Finally, you were securely fastened into your car seat, and we were on our way home for the first time with our son. The entire ride home, I looked in the rearview mirror at mom as she smiled at you, occasionally wiping your face and talking to you the whole time. I could see the pure love in mom's eyes for you, and it warmed my heart.

At that moment, all the questions and fears went away. Those emotions were replaced with the overwhelming desire to keep you safe and protect you at all costs. My doubts about being a good father were overshadowed by my desire to be the best dad I could be for you.

Son, I want the best for you, and I have always been willing to do whatever it takes to keep you safe and protect you from all harm... spiritual, physical, mental, and emotional. I may be tougher on you at times than you would like, but know that I want to give you the foundation you need to survive in this crazy and often cruel world. You should know that I will always make sure that you are buckled up.

First Bath

"Wash away your troubles with some bubbles." ~
Unknown

Bath time has always been an adventure with you son. In the early years, there had to be the right combination of temperature, toys, and bubbles or you were not happy. Nowadays the challenge is getting you to take a bath and make sure you wash behind your eyes. When I think back to the first bath I gave you, I have to admit it hasn't always been a challenge. In fact, the first bath reminded me of a special moment in my life.

You were such a little fella that we had a special tub for you, and we would put you inside the tub. I wish I knew what you were thinking because you often had a weird look on your face the whole time. If I had to guess, you were wondering what was going to happen, what the bubbles were, and hoping that we didn't let you slide into the water.

I still remember the first bath I gave you. We were in the guest bathroom in our townhouse in Virginia. Mom was busy, so I offered to bathe you myself. Prior to this, it was often a team effort with mom and me sharing in the duty of bathing you. This was my first solo bath with you, and I knew I could do it without drowning you at that point.

Everything was going as expected. The bubbles had formed, and the water was lukewarm. I had your baby soap, washcloth, and towel with the hood attached to wrap you up and keep you warm after the bath was done. Of course, you had a weird look on your face, so I felt I was doing everything correctly.

As I held the back of your head carefully and bathed you, I had a memory of my baptism when I was twelve years old. This was such a significant moment in my life that I got consumed in emotion as I bathed you. My baptism was about more than just dedicating my life to Christ. I was actually baptized at my dad's church in California. I was visiting Papa Pedro that summer, and we talked about my faith almost daily. He asked me if I had been baptized and if I wanted to do it while I was there. After calling my mom to discuss my decision, I was signed up for baptism.

Growing up without my father in my home was difficult because of the many life events he was not able to witness or talk me through. But how significant was it to share my baptism with my dad? This was truly a special moment that I was able to share with my dad. I trusted the counsel he gave me regarding my faith. As scared as I was to go through with the baptism, he calmed me and showed that he was right alongside me. As soon as I came up from the baptismal pool to get dressed, he was right there with a towel and big hug.

Son, when I finished bathing you, I sat you on my lap and wrapped you with your towel and hugged you tightly. Your first bath from me was not the spiritual moment I had with my dad, but it set me on a course to share my faith with you and to ensure that I didn't miss those special moments in your life.

I want to make sure you have that special feeling I had after my baptism whenever you suffer or accomplish things in life. I want you to look up to see me, your biggest fan, there by your side ready to embrace you with a big affirming hug.

First Steps

"Do the difficult things while they are easy and do the great things while they are small. A journey of a thousand miles must begin with a single step." ~ Lao Tzu

I have had this quote in a small picture frame on my desk for several years. It was a gift from our very special friend in Memphis. There's just so much meaning in these two sentences that I want you to understand son. When I think of the many miles you will travel in life, I reflect on the process you went through just to take your first step.

You were such a busy little fella. I remember you pulling up on the sofa so that you could stand up to see what we were doing. Once you figured out that you could scoot across the floor, you were unstoppable. You didn't bother crawling like other babies. Instead, you mastered the military crawl as if you were a soldier maneuvering across a field of bobbed wire. You always had a look of determination on your little face, and boy did you smile when you reached your destination across the room. Your crawl was very slow and methodical. So much so that I began to call you Turtle.

In just a few short months, you were no longer satisfied with the military crawl. You were determined to walk. I watched you as your little wobbly legs took steps of uncertainty while you squeezed the blood out of my fingers holding yourself upright. Often it looked as if your feet would take off without you because your legs always get out ahead of your body. I would tell you to slow down, but you never did. Your desire to walk drove you. If you lost your balance, you would simply squeeze my fingers harder until you regained your composure. Then finally, you let go.

Those first few times walking without my help were funny but tough to watch. I really didn't want to see you hurt yourself by falling, but those wobbly steps were hilarious to watch. You couldn't walk a straight line, and I was beginning to think you were made of rubber. Every time you fell down, you bounced right back up. The more you walked, the more confident you became, and the easier it was for you to walk without stumbling or falling. It was so exciting to watch.

As your dad, watching you go through the process of learning to walk, it made me think of learning to walk through life, especially in faith. It has never been and never will be easy. I have had many stumbles and uncertain steps along the way. In fact, I have even fallen several times. But just like I was there to lift you up when you fell, our Father was there to lift me up as well. I could always lean on Him just as you did with me when you felt like you might fall. He would dust me off, tell me or show me that I was ok, put me back up on my feet, and point me in the direction I needed to go.

Son, as you go through life, always remember that your Father is near and that He ordered your steps before you were conceived.

First Day

"The most important day of a person's education is the first day of school, not Graduation Day." ~ Harry Wong

The time had come for you to start preschool. Mom and I were both excited and scared to death. For the first three years of your life, you were with one of us every single day and almost every hour of each day. Now we had to put our precious gift in the hands and care of strangers. This terrified us as parents, but we knew that you would be in good, loving hands at your new school.

The first day of school came, and we were standing in your classroom as the bell rang. It was time for mom and dad to go to work and leave you there at school. You looked up at me with the saddest eyes as if you knew something was wrong... something was about to happen that you wouldn't like. I leaned over to give you a hug and a big kiss and told you how much I love you.

I knew I had to get mom out of there quickly before we both lost it. When I got in the car, mom and I prayed for your safety and protection while you were at school and away from us. All I kept picturing was your big brown eyes looking up at me. I knew that look all too well. It was the look of uncertainty. It was the look of fear. It was the look of feeling abandoned that I had as a child.

You were only in school for three hours, and I couldn't wait to rush into your classroom to pick you up that day. We got to school a little early so that we could see you playing with the other kids and to ensure that you were adjusting well. It was truly a proud dad moment to see you laughing and running around with the other kids simply enjoying life.

Then it happened. You looked up and saw mom and me looking in the window. You took off running toward the door, so excited to see us. You gave me the tightest hug ever and smiled from ear to ear. I said, "Matthew, I told you I'd be back in a little while." As the year went along, you made friends and couldn't wait to get into your classroom every morning. Your excitement for school helped us feel better about leaving you there.

As you continue to grow and find your independence, know that I'm always here with you son. Even when I'm not with you, I'm praying for you. You will always have me in your heart, so you won't be lonely.

Strong Foundation

"You're off to great places! Today is your day! Your mountain is waiting, so… get on your way!" ~ *Dr. Seuss*

The last several years as your dad have been so much fun. The best part has been watching you grow and discover the world around you. Every day, you learn something new through your experiences and in many ways I get to relive my childhood through you.

Son, I made so many mistakes along the way, and I want to ensure that you don't do the same. I know you just want to be a kid and enjoy life. I know that you are going to make mistakes. I even know that I don't have all the answers. However, I still can't help but use our experiences as teaching moments to give you guidance on making decisions, respecting others, and giving unselfishly to those in need.

As you grow into your adolescent years, you are always making me proud by making smart choices even when your friends disagree. I see how you treat your friends. I see the respect you show adults and those in authority. I see the compassion and love you show for complete strangers facing difficult times. I just pray that you always know that these are the qualities that will take you very far in life.

I'm sure the teenage years will bring new opportunities for our relationship, and I am looking forward to the challenge. You are an incredible young man with your mother's heart and a strong foundation built on faith and principles of loving others. This will sustain you in those teen moments that test your willpower and faith. Also, know that I am always here in your corner to help you sort through what life throws at you.

My next letters will be all about dating and making smart choices to respect young ladies and yourself in your teens and twenties. I think I'll start working on that now because there's so much I've learned from my mistakes over the years.

I love you son!

Dad Quotes

I hope you have enjoyed Letters 2 My Son. As I shared this concept with friends, a few offered words of wisdom they have shared with their sons.

Son, there's nothing you can do to make me stop loving you. ~ Lamar

Son, I apologize to you for being too hard on you. ~ Lamar

Grit is the single most important aspect in regards to success. Never stop working hard towards something you truly care about. No matter how many times you have to start over or overcome roadblocks. ~ Donte

Be willing to stand alone. As men we're naturally bigger and stronger than women and children. We respect women as equals, but protect them because it's our duty. There are going to be times when everyone is going in the wrong direction, or ignoring those that are going in the wrong direction. Be willing to stand strong and stand alone to do what's right. We're not serving man; we're serving God. ~ Donte

Don't start stuff. Don't take stuff. ~ Donte

Son, you are a king. Never let a woman half love you. It's ok to let her go. ~ Donte

Life is decision making, you must be willing to suffer the consequences of your decisions good or bad. ~ Kedrick

Working hard is not an option. Life is hard work. The question is what are you willing to work hard at? ~ Kedrick

About the Author

Sedrik R. Newbern is a successful business owner, author and John Maxwell Certified Coach, Trainer, and Speaker specializing in recreating relationships. When Sedrik shows up, relationships are recreated into workable, productive alliances that produce measurable results for individuals and business people. Years of experience have taught Sedrik that personal and business difficulties always stem from relationships that are stuck, burdened, and unworkable. This knowledge is what drives him to be the force that recreates relationships into something that is peaceful, productive, empowering, and prosperous.

A recognized leader in business and personal relationship coaching, Sedrik has developed and conducted hundreds of workshops, and inspirational keynotes. His keynote presentations, workshops, and consultations are interactive, thought-provoking, and life-altering. His style is authentic and engaging, and he is driven by his mission to assist people in recreating the relationships in their lives and businesses into partnerships that work.

Relationship is fundamental to every aspect of existence as a human being. When relationships are draining, resentful, unforgiving, and toxic, they become damaging to both individuals and businesses. Sedrik has an innate ability for identifying what isn't working and revealing it so that relationship can be recreated into something that is life-giving and empowering.

He serves on several non-profit boards and committees including serving as co-founder of The Precious Gift of Hope Foundation. For his leadership in business and the community, Sedrik has been recognized as one of Lake County Illinois' Most Influential African Americans, received the Alumni Achievement Award from Western Kentucky University Gordon Ford School of Business and received the Entrepreneur of the Year Award and Civic Leadership Award from the Chamber of Commerce.

A native of Nashville, TN, Sedrik holds a BS in Marketing from Western Kentucky University and an MBA with a concentration in Economics from Tennessee State University. He is the President and founder of Newbern Consulting Group, LLC as well as President of Phoenix Insurance & Financial

Services, Inc. an Allstate Insurance agency in Libertyville, IL.

Sedrik's success as an entrepreneur, he attributes to the support and motivation he receives from his wife Denise and their son Matthew.

For more information on his books, or to invite Sedrik to conduct workshops and motivational keynotes, please visit his website **www.sedriknewbern.com**.

Other Books/eBooks by Sedrik Newbern
Unconditional Forgiveness
Lessons on Letting Go To Build Better Relationships

Unpack Now
Get Rid of the Baggage in Your Relationships

How Did I Let This Happen?
5 Steps To Help You Move On

Stay connected with Sedrik:

Twitter & Instagram – @sedriknewbern
Facebook – SedrikRNewbern
LinkedIn – SedrikNewbern

www.ingramcontent.com/pod-product-compliance
Lightning Source LLC
Chambersburg PA
CBHW071801020426
42331CB00008B/2360